REAL LIVES

Humphrey Bogart

IRIS HOWDEN

ALBSU *The Basic Skills Unit*
Registered Charity No. 1003969

The name Humphrey Bogart
makes most people think
of the film *Casablanca*.

We see the night club owner, Rick,
in his white tuxedo.

A piano is playing softly.

A beautiful woman
walks out of his past
and into the bar.

Everyone knows famous lines
from *Casablanca* –
lines like "Play it again, Sam"
or "Here's looking at you, kid."

Everyone knows the famous song –
"You must remember this,
A kiss is still a kiss . . ."

Casablanca was made in 1943.

It seemed to sum up
what love in war time was all about –
a chance meeting,
a short moment of happiness
in a world gone mad.

The film won many awards,
and made a lot of money.

But it is the magic of the two stars,
Ingrid Bergman and Humphrey Bogart
that we remember today.

Early Life

For Humphrey Bogart,
success had been a long time coming.

He was born in New York
on January 23rd 1899.

His father was a doctor
and his mother an artist.
She sold pictures she had painted
of Humphrey as a child
to a baby food company.

He hated school,
and left as early as he could.

He joined the navy
when World War One broke out.
He was wounded,
and this left a scar on his lip.

After the war he did a few odd jobs.
One was stage manager in a theatre,
and soon he was doing small walk-on parts.

He was spotted by a talent scout
from the big film company,
20th Century Fox,
and he went to Hollywood.

He made 9 films – none of them very good.

He got fed up,
and went back to New York.
There he had a hit in a play
called *The Petrified Forest*.

Back to Hollywood

The successful play was made into a film,
also called *The Petrified Forest*.

Bogart played a gun-man on the run.

For years after this, he was type cast.
All he got was gangster parts.
Bogart tried to live the part off screen as well,
drinking a lot and acting tough.

His first big success
was *The Maltese Falcon*,
made in 1941.
This was a thriller,
full of crooks and gangsters
all trying to steal a valuable statue.

Bogart played the detective, Sam Spade.

This is how Bogart made his name –
as the tough guy in the raincoat
and the trilby hat.

He was always the hero,
the one who knows the difference
between right and wrong,
the only one who stays honest
right to the end of the film.

He tries to act tough,
but underneath
he's just a lonely guy
with a big soft heart.

This may explain why Bogey was so popular.
He wasn't really good looking,
like other film stars,
but he had a heart of gold.

Many people remember Bogart's voice –
handing out the wise cracks!

The Married Man

By the time he made *Casablanca*,
Bogart had been married 3 times.
His 4th marriage was to last
for the rest of his life.

In 1945 he made a film
called *To Have And Have Not*.
The girl in the film
was new to the screen.
She was 19, tall and slim, an ex-model.
She was Lauren Bacall.

She and Bogart fell for each other.
He divorced his wife to marry her.
In spite of the 25-year age gap,
they had a happy life together.
They had two children,
a boy and a girl.

They were also on screen together
in another movie, *The Big Sleep*.
Bogart played another private eye,
Philip Marlowe.

After the War

In the war years,
Bogart had made lots of action movies.
After the war,
he could choose more interesting work.

In *The Treasure Of The Sierra Madre*,
he played a miner greedy for gold.
Bogart liked this sort of part –
the born loser,
a man breaking down before our eyes.

Later, he won an award
for playing another man
having a break down –
a sea captain in *The Caine Mutiny*.

Bogart could also play comedy.

He won an Oscar for his part
as the grumpy captain of a run-down boat
in *The African Queen*.

Katherine Hepburn was his co-star,
the bossy lady who has to travel with him.

They made an unusual couple.
But of course they fell in love
before the end of the film!

The African Queen is often very funny,
as well as having some tender moments.

The *African Queen*
was 1952's top money maker.

But by this time,
Bogart only had a few more years to live.
He had cancer of the throat,
and the illness made him look tired and thin
in his later films.

He knew he was dying.

The night before his death,
instead of saying as usual – "Goodnight Kid,"
to Lauren Bacall,
he said "Goodbye Kid."

He was in such pain,
he did not sleep all night,
and he died the next morning.

The End

Bogart died on Monday January 14th 1957.

At his funeral in Beverley Hills,
all the big stars of the day
came to pay their last respects.

All except for Frank Sinatra –
he was too upset to go to the funeral.

Inside the church there were no flowers.
His widow had asked friends
to give money
to the American Cancer Society.

Instead, on the coffin
was a model of the boat he loved –
called the Santana.

Outside the church,
a crowd of 3,000 people stood
during the service.

There was a minute's
silence on all the near-by film lots in Hollywood.

It was to mark the passing
of one of Hollywood's last great stars.